Hope Was Here

Yorkshire Publishing
TULSA

ISBN: 978-1-960810-06-9
Hope was Here

Yorkshire Publishing
1425 E 41st Pl
Tulsa, OK 74105
www.YorkshirePublishing.com
918.394.2665

Published in the USA

Hope was Here

HOPE DAVIDS

CONTENTS

the unwelcome Wagon

I remember why these streets are haunted
and why the sky is grey.
This quaint little town
lives in a world of yesterdays.

If you want a macabre adventure
I'll take you all around.
Let me show you all the places
where hope was lost and found.

Sunset on River Street

I remember summer twilight
     on River Street like an old friend.
I would sit in the backyard
     and watch the sun descend.

The silence of dusk and I
     made a perfect pair
     as a soft, warm breeze
     blew through my unkempt hair.

I wondered why so many things
     in my life didn't make sense
     as I watched the sun disappear
     behind our chain-link fence.

Every night I'd say goodbye
     to my brightest, truest friend,
     but I always had faith
     that she would rise again.

Rainforest Lullaby

I remember the day
      she told me we were leaving,
      my cheeks wet
      and my chest heaving.

She promised me
      it would be good,
      that there'd be lots of playmates
      in our new neighborhood,

      but I couldn't think of anything
      that could replace what I'd had.
I didn't want a lot of playmates.
All I wanted was my dad.

"More playmates than there are trees in a rain
forest?"
      came my hesitant reply,
      and with a nod and a single tear,
      that became my hopeful lullaby.

Delusive contentment

The curtains
   might be drawn
   but I just want you to know that
   the lights are on

   in case you get tired
   of being alone,
   in case you decide
   that you want to come home.

things I Love and Hate

Telephone lines
　　　　and tearful goodbyes.

Sunsets
　　　　and restlessness.

Palm trees
　　　　and bumblebees.

Honesty
　　　　in melodies.

You.

Jigsaw Families

Maybe this one
  will finally fit,
  I think as I try
  to press myself in.

I'll sand down my edges
  and paint myself a new color.
If you don't like that one,
  I'll just choose another.

I hope you'll be happy.
I hope that you'll stay.
I hope all my baggage
  won't scare you away.

I hope none of my fuck-ups
  prove to be fatal.
I hope there's a seat
  for me at your table.

Dear Protagonist

I promise one day soon
    you'll revel in the glory.
You are not just a supporting character
    in someone else's story.

the warmth of autumn

Like a patchwork quilt,
     as dusk turns to dawn
     and I tremble with guilt,

     my greatest treasure,
     you are the stitches
     that keep me together.

Birth of a Demolition

I sit here in the shadows
    of the local shopping mall
    and hear memories of laughter
    traipsing up and down the halls.

I hear the ghosts of teenagers
    in the roller rink upstairs
    that's been shut down for years
    because they all stopped going there.

I can see the fun they had
    in the carvings on the floor
    and I wonder why no one bothered
    to come here anymore.

The darkened movie theater
    sits alone across the way
    and no one's bought a ticket
    in at least a thousand days.

The food court's empty and abandoned,
    all except the pizza place,
    but as the guy hands me my slice,
    the smile slips off of his face.

Not for long, just for a second,
    but long enough for me to see
    that once upon a time
    this was his favorite place to be.

Violent Silence

Young and innocent
    all of her life,
    she had never been touched
    and that was all right.

Then along came a boy
    she didn't know she needed,
    who could make her feel whole
    and, in the same breath, defeated.

What was once beautiful
    became detrimental
    when one night his touches
    were no longer gentle.

Frozen in fear,
    she didn't put up a fight,
    which makes the world think
    what he did was all right.

Society asks,
    "If you don't fight or scream,
    how's he supposed to know
    what you mean?"

But should she be punished
    if she wasn't even asked
    if it was all right for him
    to perform this act?

When the truth comes out,
    they're always so shocked,
    but theft is still theft
    if the door is unlocked.

Starry Night

Behind closed doors, I'm everything.
You make me shine so bright
    in the darkness of your bedroom,
    in the quiet of the night,

    but all the magic goes away
    with the arrival of the light
    when the outside world creeps in
    and suddenly I have to fight.

Fight for your attention,
    fight to remind you what we have,
    fight to keep you close to me,
    to keep us on our path.

I've come to hate the sun
    because it only comes to ruin.
Why do you only love me
    when we lay under the moon?

Imaginary Friend

Made of plastic and cloth
      with a smile painted on,
      waiting here in my house
      whenever you're gone.

Pick me up when you're bored,
      when you want to have fun.
Then cast me aside
      when you've decided you're done.

Go out and play.
I'll be waiting right here
      for the one rainy day
      that comes every few years.

Toxic Dusk

I go over our conversation again and again,
    spinning your words around in my head,
    thinking of all the things
    I wish you would have said.

Lucid craving

In a dream
> you were mine to keep
> so I beg myself
> to go back to sleep.

I'm kept awake
> so I just pretend
> I was blessed with the chance
> to see you again.

Highway 531

Tonight I'm not home.
Tonight I don't know who's in my home.
Tonight I still have a home,
       but tonight I'm not there.

Tonight my home is the asphalt I lay on.
Tonight my home is in the stars
       dangling from the early morning sky
above me,
       but tonight I'm not there.

Dawn's Remorse

I go over our conversation again and again,
        spinning our words around in my head,
        thinking of all the things
        I wish I'd never said.

Dead Letters

I thought
    my pen
    had finally run dry,
    same as my eyes.

I assumed
    that I'd
    be **pressed for** words,
    no **more** to be heard,

    but my heart finds
    the words with ease
    as my hand
    refuses to cease.

I plead and pray
    every day
    for **nothing** more
    to say

    while you
    weep and pray
    for whom
    I be**came**.

Insidious Games

It's the mist that coats your windshield
      as you're driving down the highway,
      under pitch black skies
      sprinkling you with rain.

You don't even notice at first.
It just keeps building up
      until your wiper blade gets stuck
      and suddenly you're fucked.

In the beginning, it comes
      in manageable amounts.
You let it stay because you think
      you can keep it down.

The thing is, it grows like a weed that you
      don't worry about until it grows too tall
      and you can no longer see
      the road in front of you at all.

Radioactive children

Tears fall
      as the sky turns a dark blue
      and you tell me
      everyone always leaves you.

I guess this is the part
      where I'm supposed to feel sorry for you,
      but I don't
      because everyone leaves me too.

Sweetheart,
      we are not to be pitied.
We are the toxic waste
      that flows beneath this city.

To the Boy Whose Heart I Broke under the Moonlight

it wasn't that I didn't feel.
I just wasn't ready
for something real.

Voyager

You were never supposed to fall in love
    with the girl that can't be true
    because her heart belongs to open skies
    and can't belong to you.

She'll sit with you on rooftops
    and spare a kiss or two
    but her heart belongs to open seas
    and can't belong to you.

It's nothing that you did
    and it's nothing that you are.
It's just that she needs to spend her life
    chasing her wishing star.

You were never supposed to fall in love
    with the fire in her eyes
    because darling, you'll get burned
    long before that fire dies.

Garage Bands and Lipstick-Stained Coffee Cups

In a small, dimly lit cafe,
> where we were sitting
> you looked down and saw lyrics
> that I had hand-written.

I'll never forget
> when you looked up and said
> my penmanship was beautiful,
> you could tell that my head

> was bursting with thoughts
> trying to get through to the surface,
> that my handwriting was messy
> because it was filled with purpose.

What I'm sure was
> a very small moment to you
> in that moment made me feel
> I could be beautiful too.

We Are Okay

A drink as red as sunset
    and a friend as true as you.
An honest conversation
    and a cigarette or two.

The night is dark and raw
    and the drive is long and loud
    and you make me realize it's okay
    that I stand out from the crowd.

I don't pray a lot these days,
  I don't get a lot of lucky breaks,
  and I see a lot more rain than sunshine
  in my own day to day.

But somehow
  I ended up with you
  so somehow
  I ended up in a pew

  for the first time
  in several years,
  praying on bony knees
  through my tears.

I hadn't talked to God
  in a really long time,
  but still I asked Him to help me make
you smile
  for the rest of my life.

I don't pray a lot these days
  but I finally got my lucky break,
  and I'd pray to every god there is,
  I'll pray to all of them every day

  if it means I get to love you forever
  in all of your perfect ways.
What's that?
Oh, of course you're gay.

Happily Never After

I dreamed of you
    for so long,
    immortalizing you
    in every poem and every song.

A beautiful portrait
    burned in my head,
    imagining all the things
    that you never quite said.

But then I learned the truth
    on a warm, sunny Wednesday
    and I realized I'd definitely
    made a mistake.

You're not the person
    I thought you were.
The plans in my mind
    started to morph and blur.

Curse my expectations
    for making me believe
    in a fictional persona
    you could never achieve.

I learned that day
    that people aren't magic.
A person's just a person.
How unbearably tragic.

You lit a match for me and tried to light my way
    through a darkened corridor,
    but I mistook it for a wildfire so I ran
    for the cover of darkness once more.

Huntington Ghosts

We've sat on these swings
    for so many years.
They've seen all the pain,
    the laughter and tears.

I don't think I was ready
    to say goodbye,
    to swing on these swings
    for the very last time,

    but I remember the last time.
I remember sitting here with you
    as you told me under the stars
    that you didn't know what to do.

After weeks of isolation
    the tears finally poured out
    and I realized what you needed
    couldn't come out of my mouth.

So I held onto you
    and you hung onto me
    as we tried to have faith
    in all the things we couldn't see.

Lighthouse

Happiness to me
    is like a light far out at sea
    that I can never quite reach
    as I stand on the shore, freezing in my bare feet.

Rum and Reruns

I've seen this one before,
  a constant script that never changes.
Just one more episode of the same old show.
The monotony's contagious.

I never think to change the channel
  or put on something new.
I'm always stuck in the same routine,
  in shades of grey and blue.

Broken Reflection

I watch every hope for my future
      echo silently on the floor,
      and in the pieces I see all the ghosts
      of who I was before.

In denial, I maneuver the pieces
      and try to glue everything back together,
      but I realize no matter what I do,
      I can't make this any better.

I see a million tiny versions of everything I've lost
      shining up at me,
      and the more I try to hang onto the illusion,
      the more I start to bleed.

I can look at you, I can shut my eyes,
      but I can't escape my doubts.
I can't ignore the cracks this time
      and now I'm

      bleed
      ing
      ou
      t.

Winchester Mirages

No wonder I'm high
      every moment I'm awake.
It soothes the anxiety
      that every move I make

      will be
      the wrong one.

That's how you've conditioned
      my brain to work,
      convinced it's not love
      if it doesn't hurt.

I'm always
      the wrong one.

Your way
      is the only way
      because every day,
      you're so afraid

      that I'll realize you're
      the wrong one.

You could never
      get it right
      so now you haunt
      my dreams at night.

...

Is that a gun?

Say hi to the stars
for me.

Porcelain Heart

Do you understand now?
Did I explain it well?
Why I hold my breath?
Why I walk on eggshells?

I'm just so afraid
      that you'll peel away
      these layers of paint
      and see that I'm tainted.

I'm afraid you'll get scared
      if you break down my walls,
      that you'll hand me the receipt
      because nobody wants to buy a broken doll.

Between the Walls

At this point, we're not that different,
    just separated by walls.
I can hear Cathy cuss out her husband
    and Donny shave his balls.

Each room has a story,
    both tragic and unique.
Each room also has bad insulation
    and at least two ceiling leaks.

The guy upstairs is pissed
    because life tried him but he flunked,
    and the guy next door snores so loud all night,
    we call him Captain Shitty Lungs.

But as the Captain's snoring shakes the house,
    one thing unites us all:
    the beautifully hushed chorus of laughter
    trickling between the walls.

Forgiveness

If the road to hell
    is paved with good intentions,
    the road to heaven
    is paved with second chances.

Sand castles and cigarette ashes

I wrote my name
      in the sand the other day.
Maybe it's still there or maybe
      the waves already washed it away.

I don't mind
      either way.
I left something behind,
      even if it couldn't stay.

the immaculate eviction

When your soul feels like a haunted house,
      abandoned and empty except for the spiders,
      you need to remember you're strong enough.
You were born a fighter.

The light in your eyes can outshine the darkness.
Flowers can bloom out of these walls.
Your spirit can shine through these broken windows
      as long as you have the balls.

A Love Letter

To the girl upstairs,
     the girl I don't question because I know she is brave.
To the girl with lavender hair
     who is only a child but has seen a lifetime's pain.

To the boy that lives with her
     who hides his secrets in the dark.
To the man that sits on the patio next to mine
     and plays the guitar that lights a spark

     in the eye of the man's mother,
     the mother that is the reason he plays.
To the boy who sings at the top of his lungs
     as he passes by my back door every day.

To all the stories that reside in a single building,
     and to the billions being lived across the world,
     and to you, reading this.
You are poetry.

McKinnon

Today is graduation day.
I didn't sleep at all.
I stayed awake all through the night
    staring at the wall,

    remembering the bus ride
    on a morning just like this
    on our way to school,
    never thinking that we'd miss

    the classrooms or the hallways,
    the teachers or the bus,
    believing that the world
    was out there waiting just for us.

I cannot stand the silence
    so I sneak out on the roof
    to watch the rising sun
    and to see the living proof

    that life truly waits for no one
    because all of that is gone
    and now all I have left
    is this memory of the dawn

    and the girl that sat down next to me
    on the bus that day,
    the girl who said that life goes quick
    so don't let it get away.

It's been seven years since she told me that
    and as I watch the morning light,
    I sit and smoke a cigarette
    and realize she was right.

Bluebird Symphony

I'll never know the pain you felt
 from half the world away
 but I know your story wasn't meant
 to end that fateful day.

Millions of voices laughing
 couldn't make you want to stay
 so now millions of voices are crying
 over things you wouldn't say.

I feel the dial tone
 and the empty seat at the dinner table.
I feel the weight of it
 even though you just weren't able.

I wish you were still here
 so that you could hear my voice
 telling you it's not the end,
 saying there's a better choice.

Last call

Look at us out here,
      navigating these crazy lives,
      rowing weak ships
      and praying they don't capsize,

      fleeing old
      familiar nests,
      searching for answers
      in the wicked unrest,

      desperately trying
      to keep our heads above water,
      to prepare our sons
      and protect our daughters.

Ladies and gentlemen,
      this is our drinking song.
If you know the words,
      feel free to sing along.

Waxing Gibbous

Depression is like sitting on your back steps
     and gazing longingly at the moon.
One moment, you can see it
     and the next, the clouds obstruct the view.

Suddenly there's no moon in your sky
     and you start to get really scared.
If you're lucky, you can find a way to remember
     the fact that your moon is there.

But please don't look down on the unlucky ones
     that forget about their moons
     before they're snuffed out forever,
     the ones who forget there's always room

     for every single moon
     in this giant lovely fog,
     but I cannot rescue them
     so I'll leave you with this epilogue:

When the cuts run too deep
     and the waves feel too high,
     even if you can't see it, always remember
     there is forever a moon in your sky.

eternal blizzard, eternal sun

Anxiety can feel like
     a long New England winter.
The road ahead of you looks bleak and unwel-
coming,
     and the ice under your feet keeps getting
thinner.

Every step you take,
     your feet are slipping out from under
you.
Everywhere's dark and slick with ice
     and you don't think you can make it
through.

You struggle minute by minute
     just to find your traction,
     but you're too scared of the outcome
     to take decided action.

But the next morning, when you see the sun
     and the roads are clear once more,
     you know you have another chance
     to do better than before.

You know that it's not over.
Another storm will come,
     but right now, you have this moment.
Right now, you have the sun.

Growing Pains

I leave the bookstore
    in the pouring rain,
    tuck my book in my jacket,
    my shift finished for the day.

The wind whips my face
    as I make my way
    to the candy shop
    that just opened yesterday.

It's warm and bright
    as the bell dings behind me
    and I maneuver through a
    gumdrop and lollipop sea.

The girl behind the counter
    gives me chocolate covered pretzels
    and has no idea that later,
    they'd cater a bittersweet festival

    as I sit on my bed,
    the salt stinging my tongue
    because I remember the way
    we used to stay up

way past our bedtime,
    telling stories and jokes
    and trying hard not
    to wake up our folks.

The salt on my tongue
    stings the wounds in my heart
    that ache because we're
    three hundred miles apart.

Gas Station Blues

It's a Sunday
    just like the last
    and the one before that,
    and the one before that.

Overworked
    and underpaid
    is the insidious mantra
    that echoes through my veins.

I plug the aux cord
    into my phone
    but I need to get gas
    before I can go home.

Exhausted and empty,
    I pull up to the pump
    that declines my card
    and I wish I could numb

    the bubbling rage
    as it reaches my head.
I wish it'd just stay
    where I hid it instead.

So I go in to see the cashier
    with a sigh
    but I'm immediately disarmed
    when she looks in my eyes.

She says, "*Wow,*
    that's a beautiful tattoo."
She catches me off guard
    so I just say, "Thank you."

Despite what had happened
    and the day I'd just had,
    I got back in my car
    and I wasn't so mad.

Ode to Direct Deposit

I'm very tired
    and very stoned,
    and I would like
    to go the fuck home.

Give me my money
    so I can buy something green
    and find the world funny
    to get through another week.

Afterglow

Before I met you,
    my soul made a home
    in a dark mausoleum,
    incomplete and alone.

A permanent residence
    in a haunted past.
A graveyard of brokenness
    and love that won't last.

Then you walk in with this candle,
    the tiniest flame
    shines out of all my darkest places
    every single day.

christmas on Main street

My heart is full as we sit
    in your brand new home,
    the one that you've curated
    all on your own,

    eating takeout
    from the restaurant downstairs
    with a box as a table
    and some bean bag chairs,

    bathed in the glow
    of the Christmas lights
    that still illuminate
    our February nights,

    listening to the hum
    of the traffic below
    as the snow falls gently
    past your windows.

There's still joy in my heart
    whenever you're near
    because the holidays might be gone,
    but we are still here.

Ice Cream Run

It started out
>	as a simple errand,
>	a late night trip
>	to see a friend

then a stop
to get some ice cream,
but as we start
to descend

down a dirt hill with our windows down
and summer in our hearts,
I realize love matters a whole lot more
than the miles you're apart.

The Ballad of Two Spoons

One for me,
        one for you

        when we went to TGI Friday's
        on a Monday
        for my birthday.

We ordered one rainbow cake
        but the guy gave us two spoons.
He knew.

Now we're laying in bed
        and I'm wrapped up in you
        and I fit in your arms perfectly,
        two spoons.

Final Draft

Someone once asked
    to read something I'd written,
    but I told her she'd have to wait
    for the revision.

She didn't think
    if I changed up my words,
    she'd receive the message
    I meant to be heard.

But hear me now, ma'am,
    as loud as a church fart,
    sometimes the revision
    is the most important part.

Remember the christmas lights

when love was new
and everything was all right.

During the darkest night,
        when the weight is too heavy,
        remember the Christmas lights.

With my truth,
    I write
    in the hopes that my darkness
    can be someone else's light.

With this pen,
    I fight.
This pen is my weapon against
    the harshness of this life.

I refuse to be consumed
    by the darkness in my head.
I will make beauty from ashes
    if it takes me 'til I'm dead.

Though this valley's long and dark,
    I will walk it with no fear
    and I will pave the way in love
    so they will all know hope was here.